Just Words

A collection of short poems

By
Keith Hearn

ISBN-13:978-1721170388
ISBN-10:1721170383

Writing poetry is like writing short stories

If my writing inspires others to write, anything, I feel I have achieved what I set out to do

*My book of poetry is dedicated to my children
Sara-Ann and Paul*

*To my grandchildren
Caitlin, Chloe, Josh and Bella*

Be free to write whatever you want

Be Inspired

Take no notice of those who want to knock anything you want to do in life

Be creative and enjoy the experience

Just be yourself

Be who you really are

Just Words

OUT OF THE BLUE

*Does it matter who or what
we are or who we have true
feelings for?*

*If we can bring love and
happiness into one another's
lives*

*Truth, honesty, trust and love
is what really matters surely*

*Love can appear suddenly
from out of the blue*

*Have faith and just see where
the journey can take's you*

Life is full of surprises

<u>SOFT</u>

*I see from your many
pictures a sultry and erotic
lady and someone who is
comfortable with their own
body*

*Your lips look so inviting
when covered in the deep red
lipstick and your eyes are
alive and full of mischief*

*Your skin looks smooth and
very soft to the touch*

Your tattoos help to enhance
your look
The simple picture of your
peach shaped bottom sets so
many men's pulses racing

MAGNET

Are my feelings forbidden
feelings?

I mean you no harm

It's just I had never known I
could ever feel this way about
you

You're like a magnet and I
am the metal filings which
attach themselves to you

All you have to say to me is "back off" and I shall leave you in peace

CLICKED

*Life is not like having a book
where a story just flows along
and is so easy to read*

*Sometimes things just happen
and can stop you in your
tracks*

*I have always known you
were around but never gave
you a second thought*

*That was until one day
something just clicked into
place and to me it made sense*

11

I messaged you thinking you would tell me to stop messaging

Luckily you didn't, and your lack of action shocked me

I must admit I had never messaged anyone like I have with you

I placed my feelings for you in print

Let's see if you do join me on the journey of life.

YOU NOW HAVE MY FULL ATTENTION

I will never be able to understand why I am with you?

Time and time again I have wracked my brain to find a reason why you are with me

Your kindness towards me is overwhelming

There is one thing I do know, and it is this, if you did not like my attention towards

*you, there has been enough
time to have told me*

*I love the attention you
shower me with*

*Life has taken on a new
meaning*

<u>*PICTURES*</u>

*Photographs suddenly appear
of you and I know you are
aware I see them*

*A certain picture grabbed
my attention*

*The bright vibrant colours
have blended in with a small
tattoo of a flower on your
arm*

*The picture reminded me of a
perfect peach. I told you
what I thought of your*

picture and yet you kept it
online for me to see

There is so much you could do
to keep me away, it seems to
me at some point you wished
for me to remain in contact
with you

LAID BARE

*I do not know what has come
over me recently*

*I have never messaged
anyone before to lay my
feeling bare and raw*

*At first, I assumed I shook
you to the very core. But on
reflection perhaps you have
always known?*

*In my mind you are so
beautiful and yet so young*

*What right do I have to come
along and to then upset your
routine
The answer is obviously none*

A very selfish gesture

TIME

You bring rays of sunshine
into other people's lives

Anyone can see how strong
you are but there again we
all have off days

Away from the crowds we all
have our own time, time for
ourselves

On our own in our own world
who do we have to bring a
ray of sunshine into our own
lives

19

Time again others rely on you to bring that brilliant ray of sunshine into their lives

Who brings the sunshine to you?

THE PERSON YOU ARE

Why would anyone wish to treat you the way you have been treated?

Mind games are not the way to treat anyone no matter what

You say they want you back, is that because they see that you are getting on with your life and you have no need to rely on them anymore

Just Words

*Your pictures show your
natural beauty for all to see*

<u>STRENGTH</u>

*For someone so young you
have such an air of maturity*

*To show such courage and
strength puts many to shame*

*You put your children first
where many do not*

Your life is your children

*You have gone through so
much in your life*

*Do not forget there is always
someone who cares*

SUNSHINE

*There you are standing so
close to me*

*A person who radiates
happiness holding my stare*

*You are a person of such
beauty*

*Such a pleasant lady and so
vibrant and full of joy*

*Ah well one can only dream
there is no harm in that is
there?*

EERILY QUITE

*The streets are eerily devoid
of vehicles and people*

*The area looked like a ghost
town*

*The scene was very like a
1960's science fiction film*

*Could the country have come
under an attack?*

*Suddenly from gardens and
inside of so many houses and
of course pubs a shout which*

so loud erupted and the noise
reverberated onto the empty
streets

The noise pierced the still air
all because the England
football team having scored a
goal during the world cup in
Russia

BELIEVE

The 2018 world cup who
would have believed at the
start of the competition
England would end up doing
so well

There was a time across the
land the England supporters
began to believe in the squad
and what they stood for

There was a point during the
world cup many began to
think "Football was coming
home"

Pride brimmed over in bucket loads and most of the country began to believe

Come on England

THE HIGHS AND LOWS

Can life ever pickup and
become like other people's
lives

Or are they just making out
that they have a better life
than you?

Life has its many ups and
downs

Sometimes the ups take much
longer to climb

*Because at the bottom looking
up can seem like climbing
mount Everest*

*It is almost impossible to
climb but climb it we must*

"OH NO"

"Oh no, that's not what I
meant, no you are not
listening to me"

Oh, how everyone laughed

"what are you all laughing
at" as he placed a hand on his
hip

His wife looked at her
husband with a hand on his
hip and she smiled

*Once again, he spoke "no
come on no one is listening to
what I have got to say"*

*"oh no, you don't understand
what I am trying to say"*

*The people standing around
him calmed down and began
to listen to what he had to
say*

<u>*SMILER*</u>

*Oh, how the young Scottish
lady has grown up*

*From her photographs she
looked full of joy*

*Always with a smile on her
face*

*Look deeply into her eyes and
there is a slight tinge of
sadness*

*Oh, how is it a Scot is living
in the principality of Wales*

Surely a contradiction in terms?

A truly loving, caring and lovely lady

With whom others seem to enjoy hurting

A BEAUTIFUL PERSON

How much fun you bring to
your family

Such a big and kind heart

A heart which has been
stabbed so many times

How you manage to keep
going is amazing

You make me smile at your
many posts on social media

You truly enjoy your social life

And at the same time your love for your family is inspiring

<u>STALKER</u>

Now not everyone can ever
boast of having a stalker

Perhaps your stalker fancies
you

You know it is another
woman

You are very attractive so
perhaps she has a crush on
you

You are very fit in both
meanings of the word

You could do far worse

Embrace the attention

THE ANCIENT CITY

How much the city has
changed it isn't the place it
was

The Romans and the
Normans went on to change
it beyond all recognition,
they also helped to build it

So many new houses have
sprung up from nowhere and
sometimes in places a house
should never be built

The city centre and the areas
around the railway station
are soon to be flattened and
once again built on with
modern monstrosities

Some call it progress others
call it architectural
vandalism

Perhaps people in twenty
years' time will reflect on the
cities past and possibly think
the same? Only time will tell

Historians will look back on
what the council has allowed

to be built and in the name of
progress

They will write about the
vandalism which has been
allowed to be carried out
within such an historic city

The Roman's when living in
the city built much of the city

To be followed by the
Normans who destroyed the
Saxon old minister and built
their Norman cathedral
which is still standing today

Thank our lucky stars some modern planner has not been allowed to run amok on the cathedral and its grounds

TRAVELLING THROUGH TIME

Life has many stages on its
journey

There are so many stops and
starts

The term "on the bus and off
the bus" is apt to the journey
I now find myself on

Life itself has a habit of
stopping and starting once
again

When will the bus finally
arrive at its destination

Where is paradise does
anybody know?

I don't know do you?

A THING OF SUCH BEAUTY

Your paintings are bright
and vibrant

The results stand out from
the canvass

You work so hard on your
work

Your friend Lulu has recently
come into your life and she
give's back to you such love
but asks for nothing in return

Expect for her food it is very a small price to pay for the happiness she gives you in return

<u>WHO ARE YOU</u>

Why would anyone wish to
treat you the way they have
treated you in the past?

Mind games are not the way
to treat anyone no matter
what

You say they want you back
is it because they you not
needing them anymore they
see you getting on with your
life

You haven't come running
back to him

Your pictures show so much
of your beauty for everyone
to see
I feel so lucky to have been
accepted for who I am

I would never hurt you

You have helped me in such a
way you will never realise

<u>EMBARRESSMENT</u>

*I should never have told you
how I felt about you*

*Sometimes it is far better to
keep one's feelings to oneself*

*I felt the ground opening and
wanting the ground to
swallow me up*

*I have never felt so
embarrassed*

*Thankfully you put me at
ease*

Not many would be as kind

SUNSHINE

There you were standing so
close to me

Such a beam of sunshine
cascading around the room

You held my stare

You are a person of such
beauty

Such a pleasant person full of
joy and vibrance

Once again someone who is so
young

Ah well one can only dream
as there is no harm in
dreaming

Well is there?

A BEAUTIFUL DAY

I apologise far too much it is a very bad habit, only because I attract bad and very horrible people I don't know what people want from me

I like you and do not know if I am living a dream suddenly you will be gone, disappear, as quickly as you arrived

I have over the years pushed so many people away, it is so easy to do, then there is no heartbreak in my life

I saw a picture of you in a restaurant and your eyes show your soul and it is full of kindness and warmth

You show much kindness towards me, I am not used to such kindness, as over the years I questioned acts of kindness

Recently I have found my broken heart has mended, finally

DROWNING

I often feel I am drowning in self doubt

Can looking back make someone stop looking forward to the future

For so many years life seems to have stagnated in the past

How can someone move on from the past?

To allow what the future many hold and to allow the future to flood into a dark world

The future is bright and is full of great delights

Move away from the darkness and begin to let the light back in

WHAT HAPPENED

Why are you the way you are

Such a beautiful person both inside
and out

What on earth happened to you to
make you the way you are

Who hurt you

It is time for you to place your
trust in someone else

It is the small steps which make up
the giant leap of faith

Maybe one day you will find true happiness

Without any strings or conditions

True happiness

THE BUTTERFLY

The butterfly flies from one flower
to another

Always on the move and never
settling

Until it finds the right spot and
then opens its wings to warm them
in the direct sunlight

The butterfly is such a graceful
creature

Myth has it they are the souls of
the dear departed

<u>LIFE</u>

Life can be so cruel

On a high when all is going so well
in life

But such a drop when life takes a
dive

It may take many years to once
again be on such a high

Never stay on a low for long as it
will drag you to the depths

<u>*FOROE ISLANDS*</u>

Such a far away place tiny Islands on the map

I have often wondered why my great grandfather Peter left such a beautiful place

The Islands are like a bright candle flickering in the darkness

The Islands are lashed by the seas and can be a precarious place to live

Such tiny Islands amid the oceans

THE SHADOW

The shadow has constantly
followed me in everything I do in
life

My life seems to have been
strangled by the shadow

I have never been able to grow to
my potential it has been hampered
by you

I wake having been suffocated by
your shadow

*I am determined one day to throw
the monkey off my back*

*To grow into the person, I was
meant to be*

THE ENCYLOPAEDIA

He is like an encyclopaedia no
matter what is said he plucks a
statistic out from the air

Many respond "I didn't know
that"

His response is hmmm hmmm it is
true

Once again, he seems to be always
correct his statistic is right on the
nail

*He never boasts instead he places
his hand onto his hip*

THE GOLFER

In he walks straight up to the bar
looking very red

The shout goes up "been playing
golf then"?

No, I am red because I have been
indoors all day?

What do you think I have been
doing in the sun and heat?

With that he supped his glass of ice
cold lager

MOTHER EARTH

How long will nature off taking
the abuse humans have inflicted
on her body

Her soul is all loving

Humanity hasn't seen her ugly
side yet?

She will fight back, and woe betide
any government who think they
can hold natures wrath at bay

The planet is covered in so much
concrete and tarmac it will mean

absolutely nothing as soon as the
fires erupt from the bowels of the
earth

The fire will destroy all the
manmade concrete and tarmac

The natural world will once again
reign supreme

Will nature ever allow humanity
to be the custodians of the natural
world again?

Who knows

We all must change our ways
before it is far too late

<u>*you*</u>

Where are you lately?

I would see you whenever you came for a meeting

You look tall and even taller in your high heals

You would dress so smart along with your designer bags with the cuddly toys hanging from the zip of your bags

A lady of such refinement and not shy of talking

*Suddenly you seem to have
dropped from the face of the earth*

Was it something I said?

THE WEATHER

The hot weather always reminds me of my childhood living in an industrial city in the North of England

The sun beating down on the tarmac roads which criss-crossed the back to back housing estates very close to the docks

Not many families could afford a holiday and would visit New Brighton beach across the River Mersey or travel as far as Blackpool

A foreign trip was to the Great Orme or the pier in Llandudno in Wales

Halcyon days

EARLY MORNING

*It is a sound which makes the start
to my day such a joy*

The sun is high in the sky

*The birds are singing in the
morning sky*

*The bees are collecting pollen from
the sun flowers*

*Butterflies are fluttering on the
gentle wind*

FROM A DISTANCE

From the gentle rolling hills the
farmer's fields sprawl for miles
around

If I could paint I would sit and
paint the scene laid out before me

I could spend my day sketching
and painting

Laid out before me are so many
greens and browns

The sky looks so blue with white
clouds high above the sky

A stream can be seen meandering between the fields one minute the thin blue line can be seen and then disappears within the many dips in the ground

The stream is of a totally different tone of blue than the blue of the sky

Such a beautiful scene

SO MUCH TO GIVE

*It is so sad to know someone has so
much to give to another*

But it is not to be

I have so much to give to someone

It takes two to share

*It sad of todays world people want
a designer partnership*

*People are what counts it is what
is in the heart not on a mobile
phone*

TRAINS

*As the train entered the station at
the end of its long journey the
noise of the steam escaping into
the air fills the platform*

*Water spewing from under the
steam engine such a sight and the
noise and smells of the old
locomotive filling the air*

*The noise of the railway men
uncoupling the carriages to hook
them up with another steam
engine further up the track to take*

the passengers on their onward journey

The steam engine at the front of the carriages had completed its journey

It waited to be filled with water and yet more coal to be loaded onto its fire tender for yet another journey

The noise and smells have never left my thoughts

A bygone age

THE FLY

It is such an annoyance

A fly has managed to get into the
room

Trying to encourage it to fly out of
one of the open windows is a waste
of time

It is time to use the fly killer

The problem is soon eradicated

GOODBYE

*The little girl was almost five and
she was very scared standing on
the platform and all alone*

*She was told to bring her
belongings all she had were the
clothes she was stood up in*

*She had her gas mask hanging by
a piece of string from her neck*

*No one from her family saw her
off from the train station*

It would be five years before she would see her family again

In that time away, her father had sadly passed away

She didn't recognise her mother because it had been so long since she had last seen her

Life for the little girl was going to change not in a very good way

BLISS

*Bliss is when I am thinking about
what I should write next*

Inspiration is all around me

*Be it taking photographs of bees in
flight or watching nature*

*The fields surrounding the village
are teaming with wild animals*

*Be they deer, birds of pray or
foxes scurrying across the farmers
fields*

Love is such a powerful word

It is a word not to be used lightly
or in a frivolous manner or in a
throwaway manner

It means so much to those who
have waited for it to come back
into their lives

Made in the USA
Columbia, SC
09 August 2018